D0337638

Roadside Bicycle Repairs

The simple guide to fixing your bike

Rob van der Plas

Illustrated by the author

Bicycle Books – San Francisco

Copyright © Rob van der Plas, 1987
First printing, 1987
Second printing, 1988

Printed in the United States of America

Cover photograph by Stief

Published by:
Bicycle Books (Publishing), Inc.
P.O. Box 2038
Mill Valley, CA 94941

Distributed to the book trade by:
(USA) Kampmann & Co., New York, NY
(Canada) Raincoast, Vancouver, BC

Library of Congress Cataloging in Publication Data:
Van der Plas, Robert, 1938 –
Roadside Bicycle Repairs
The simple guide to fixing your bike
Bibliography: p. Includes Index
1. Bicycles and bicycling, Handbooks, Manuals, etc.
2. Authorship
I. Title
Library of Congress Catalog Card Number 87–70731
ISBN 0-933201-16-8

Printed in the United States of America

Table of Contents

Table of Contents

Table of Contents

Chapter 1
Know Your Bike

The present book is a simple bicycle repair guide, to help you solve the most frequently occurring problems while you're out riding the bike. It is not meant to be a complete guide to bicycle maintenance. With the help of these instructions, you will usually be able to get back on the bike quickly after it develops a problem. Nothing more, nothing less. That, however, is what most novice cyclists – and quite a number of more experienced riders – want to know most of all.

For those who want to know more about the bicycle and its maintenance, there are bigger books on the market, such as my *Bicycle Repair Book*. For perhaps 90 percent of the problems you'll encounter, including really all those you can eliminate by the roadside, the present book is the answer and allows even the person who is not technically inclined to help himself.

The bicycle is a simple machine. Everything on it is light and straightforward enough to be understood and overhauled by even the relatively inept. So it is curious to observe how even many technically sophisticated people panic when their bikes develop a problem. Folks who don't hesitate to handle technically complex machines often think of nothing except hitching a ride home, whereas the defect could be repaired in very little time and with very simple tools. Carry those tools and a few spares, as listed in Chapter 2, together with this book in your handlebar or saddle bag, to make sure you get back as cheerfully as you leave on every bike trip.

It's largely a matter of knowing you can do it yourself. But it is also a matter of being adequately prepared. Without a pump and a few basic tools, even a technical genius can't fix a flat. And without knowing how a derailleur works or how the handlebars are clamped in, you may have a hard time getting the one to shift properly or the other to stay in the right orientation – even if you have the finest tools on the market.

These are the subjects that will be addressed in these first few chapters, before we get down to the step-by-step instructions for solving individual mechanical problems starting in Chapter 4. First we will take a closer look at the bicycle in general and your bike in particular. In Chapter 2 we'll consider the essential tools, both the general tools and those that are designed specifically for use with your bike. Then, in Chapter 3, you will be shown how to give the bike just enough basic care to prevent most serious problems from the outset.

In the remaining chapters of the book, you will find quite detailed instructions for handling specific repairs once you have established what is wrong and what has to be done about it. You may be tempted to tuck the book in your handlebar or saddle bag and forget about it until a defect does develop. That's up to you. Just the same, it will be fair to warn you that you will have an easier time of it if you take the trouble to go through the first few chapters before you set out on your first ride.

Familiarize yourself with the methodology of the book, use it to get acquainted more intimately with

1. Know Your Bike

your bike and to select the right tools to help you out. Consult it to determine what kind of simple preventive maintenance you can easily carry out yourself to keep your machine fit. That way you will have fewer breakdowns and you'll be able to ride with more confidence. You'll be a more competent cyclist; you'll also get more enjoyment and less frustration out of riding your bike.

Types of Bikes

Although in recent years only two types – the drop-handlebar derailleur bike and the mountain bike – have constituted the majority of all the bicycles sold in the US, there are other types of machines: utility bikes, real racing bikes, English type three-speeds, BMX bikes. Just the same, there is some justification for my decision to base most of the illustrations in this book on the recently more popular types of machines.

Before we get down to it, though, I shall briefly describe the various bikes available. In this context, you will find here an illustration and a brief text highlighting the most characteristic features for each of the bicycle types used on the road.

Mountain Bike

Also known as ATB (all terrain bike), shown in Fig. 1.1. Fat tires, wide handlebars, 15-speed derailleur gearing, heavy-duty brakes and a quick-adjusting saddle are the features of this rugged machine.

Fig. 1.1. Mountain bike

Ten-Speed

Though on the one hand many other bicycle models also have ten-speed gearing, while many of these machines actually have a different number of gears, ten-speed has become the most common name for these machines, shown in Fig. 1.2. It's the regular derailleur-geared bike with drop handlebars and relatively narrow saddle.

Racing Bike

No separate illustration: to the casual observer, this machine looks just like the last item. To the initiated it's a lighter and more sophisticated machine with more precise components.

Fig. 1.2. Ten-speed

1. Know Your Bike

Fig. 1.3. Utility bike

Touring Bike

The rugged equivalent of the two preceding models, and looking similar enough not to justify a seperate illustration. Equipped with accessories to carry luggage, relatively sturdy wheels and tires and not built for speed as much as the racer, this is essentially a high-quality machine, usually equipped with fifteen speeds.

Utility Bike

The old heavy American klunker, shown in Fig. 1.3. Still fondly remebered by many of my generation, but to all intent and purpose superseded by more agile and comfortable machines. Fat tires, wide handlebars, coaster brake and no gears are the usual attributes.

Fig. 1.4. Three-speed

Three-Speed

Something akin to the last item but equipped with a hub gearing mechanism, illustrated in Fig. 1.4. Getting rare these days, but they are still around, certainly in Britain, where they have always been the knockabout for the family.

Tandem

The bicycle built for two, shown in Fig. 1.5. Has made a resurgence in recent years and can be had in all different categories, though most typically equipped similarly to the ten-speed.

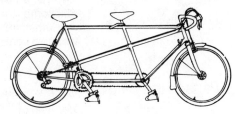

Fig. 1.5. Tandem

Folding Bike

Even rarer, with just one example shown in Fig. 1.6. Small wheels and a multiple of different designs to solve the problem of portability. Possible equipment ranges from one end of the scale to the other.

Fig. 1.6. Folding bicycle

1. Know Your Bike

15

Fig. 1.7. BMX-Bike

BMX-Bike

The kid's mountain bike, shown in Fig. 1.7. More a toy than a bike to my mind, but there's no denying that some folks cover significant distances and ride the most inhospitable terrain with these small-wheeled vehicles.

Parts of the Bike

Once you have established just what kind of bike you have, take a closer look at it. The anatomy of a typical bicycle is illustrated in Fig. 1.8. Though the model illustrated is a typical ten-speed bike, the components shown on it are also present on just about any other model – they just look a little different on one model than on the other.

Then there are some other variations, such as hub gearing, as opposed to the derailleur gearing shown, and hub or coaster brakes, as opposed to the rim brakes illustrated. Don't let that distract from the purpose of this drawing. Just examine your own bike and compare it to the one shown, learning to identify the various components on your bike by

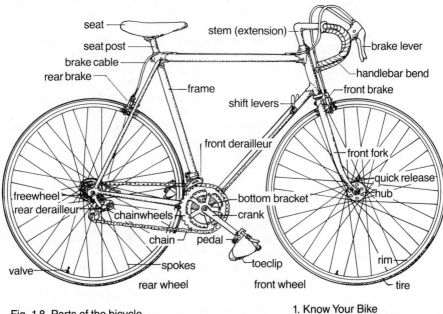

seat —
stem (extension) —
seat post —
brake cable —
brake lever —
rear brake —
handlebar bend —
frame —
front brake —
shift levers —
front derailleur —
front fork —
quick release —
hub —
freewheel —
rear derailleur —
chainwheels —
bottom bracket —
crank —
chain —
pedal —
valve —
toeclip —
spokes —
rim —
rear wheel —
front wheel —
tire —

Fig. 1.8. Parts of the bicycle

1. Know Your Bike

their proper names. That will make it infinitely easier to follow the instructions in the chapters that follow.

The simplest way to memorize the component designations and to understand the working of your bicycle is by thinking of the bike as an overall system, consisting of various functional systems: frame, steering, saddle, drivetrain, gearing, wheels, brakes and accessories. In the following section, we shall briefly summarize the function and the components of each of these systems. Consult the illustration Fig. 1.8 while we do so. One can distinguish the following functional groups:

The frame

This is the bicycle's tubular 'backbone', to which all the other components are attached. It is made up of tubular steel members and consists of the main frame, comprising top tube, seat tube and head tube, and the rear triangle, comprising nearly parallel sets of seat stays and chain stays. The various tubes are generally connected by means of lugs, while the points where the wheels are installed are referred to as drop-outs or fork-ends. Nothing normally goes wrong with the frame while you are out cycling – and if something should happen, there's little you can do about it. Consequently I have not devoted a repair chapter to the subject.

The steering system

It is required for balance and control. It comprises the front fork and the handlebar bend with its adjustable stem, as well as the headset bearings with which the system is pivotted in the frame's head tube. Repair and maintenance problems with the steering system are covered in Chapter 4.

The saddle

Your major point of contact with the bike. It is installed by means of an adjustable seat post that attaches it to the frame's seat tube. Little will go wrong, but you may have to adjust the saddle, shown in Chapter 5.

The drivetrain

That is the system that transmits the rider's effort to the rear wheel. It comprises the crankset (cranks and bottom bracket bearings, installed in the frame's lowest point, referred to as bottom bracket), pedals, chain and the freewheel assembly with sprockets on the rear wheel. The subject of drivetrain problems and the maintenance operations involved are covered in Chapter 6.

The gearing system

It allows the rider to adapt the transmission ratio to the terrain conditions. On most bikes it comprises front and rear derailleurs, as well as the shift levers and cables for their actuation. Gearing problems are amongst the most common and Chapter 7 is devoted to their solution.

The wheels

The final link between you and the road. Each wheel is an assembly made up of a central hub that rotates on ball bearings around a fixed axle installed in the frame, a set of spokes to keep it under tension, a rim and the tire mounted on the rim, and itself comprising an inner tube and a tire cover. The wheels may give you a lot of hardship, and the various repairs involved are outlined in Chapter 8.

They allow you to control your speed by decelerating the bike when the going speed doesn't allow you to handle the situation. On virtually all bikes they consist of front and rear rim brake mechanisms with brake blocks that grab the sides of the rim, together with the brake levers mounted on the handlebars and the cables which connect levers and brakes. Chapter 9 is devoted to the repair operations needed for brake problems.

Different accessories may or may not be present on any particular bike. Typical items include luggage racks, fenders, lights, reflectors, a kick stand and various other more or less useful embellishments. Chapter 10 gives some hints on assuring the accessories remain operational.

Choice of Words

Let me conclude this chapter with a few words on the subject of language and terminology. In the first place, you may already have noticed I use the masculine form of address: he, him, his. It's done to avoid clumsy constructions.

Secondly, a word about the spelling of the English language. Though this book is sold on both sides of the Atlantic, I shall adhere to American spelling within the limits of my own tolerance for some of the curious mutilation of the English language that may sometimes be noticed in other writings. Wherever common usage in Britain differs by more than the spelling, I shall explain the concept in both British and American terminology the first time it occurs.

Chapter 2
Basic Tools

It is entirely possible to carry out most of the repairs you may ever encounter with a very elementary set of tools that are cheap enough to buy and light enough to carry along on the bike. This brief chapter will introduce those essential tools.

When selecting tools, make sure you get high quality items and expect to pay a fair price. Don't be fooled by terms like 'economy tools', which is merely a polite term for shoddy junk. Quality tools are expensive. But in the long run they'll be infinitely more economic than cheaper items, since they not only last much longer, but also avoid doing damage to the parts you are working on.

Tools for bicycle use can be distinguished into two categories: general tools and bicycle-specific items, sold only at bike stores. Though a few bike shops also offer good general tools, I recommend buying those only at specialized hardware shops.

Fig. 2.1. Crescent wrench

When in doubt about the quality of either type, select the most expensive of several superficially similar looking items.

In the following parts of this chapter I have only included those tools that you can reasonably carry along on the bike. There are numerous other general and specific tools that may be useful for one job or the other, and some of the repairs described in subsequent chapters are actually better conducted with such specialized tools. However, the tools listed here will allow you to do the essential work, without loading you down unreasonably.

General Tools

Take along the general tools listed below, in the sizes indicated. Note that virtually all bicycle components use metric standard, which references the width across flats in mm.

Crescent wrench (adjustable spanner to my British readers) 6 or 8 inches long (Fig. 2.1). Try to get a model that is relatively thin and has little 'play' between the two parts of the beak.

Srewdriver with a short 4–5 mm (5/32 to 3/16 in) wide blade and a relatively short handle.

Small needle-nose pliers with a sharp cutting device.

Set of open-ended or box wrenches (spanners) in sizes ranging from 7 mm to 14 mm.

Fig. 2.2. Allen key

Set of Allen keys. These are L-shaped hexagonal rods that fit inside the head of the recently increasingly popular bolts with corresponding heads with a hexagonal recess (Fig. 2.2). Sizes of 4, 5, 6 and sometimes 7 and 8 mm will usually suffice, though some bikes may be equipped with the odd item of a smaller or in-between size.

A sharp knife. Any good pocket knife will do, though a Swiss Army knife may actually suffice to serve a multitude of other purposes as well.

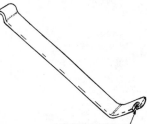

FITS AROUND SPOKE

Fig. 2.3. Tire iron

Bicycle Tools

Depending on the bike you ride, you may need a number of tools, some of which are specifically designed for the make in question. These will be covered below, following the descriptions for the

2. Basic Tools

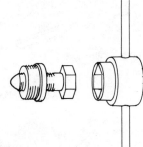

Fig. 2.4. Crank tool

Fig. 2.5. Spoke wrench

more common bicycle tools that every cyclists should carry.

A tire pump. Depending on the kind of valves used on your bike's tires, get one to fit either the big diameter Schrader valve or the small diameter Presta valve. If in doubt, ask at the bike shop.

Set of three tire irons (tyre levers), shown in Fig. 2.3. They should be thin, so they easily fit under the tire bead without damaging either the tire, the rim or the tube. If you ride a bike with tubular tires (also referred to as sew-ups in the US, tubs in Britain), you need at least a spare tire instead of these tire irons.

Tire patch kit. It should contain adhesive patches, rubber solution, an abrasive device and talcum powder. For tubular tires you can get a special set and still pray you never need it, i.e. that you never get more flats on any one trip than the number of spare tires you carry.

If your bike has so-called cotterless cranks (ask at the shop if you don't know), you will need a crank tool to match the particular make and model (Fig. 2.4).

Spoke wrench (nipple spanner), to fit the spoke nipples used on your bike's wheels (Fig. 2.5).

Chain tool, used to separate the chain (Fig. 2.6). This is a borderline tool: most cyclists would not carry one around, while others do.

Special brake wrench, if required to center or adjust the brakes used on your bike (another borderline tool).

Hub wrenches (cone spanners), which are very thin open-ended spanners, in the sizes needed for your hubs (another borderline tool, perhaps only useful for a very long trip).

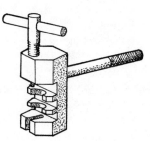

Fig. 2.6. Chain tool

Spare Parts

Carry the following spare parts, to assure you can actually replace broken items:

A couple of spokes of the right length for the front wheel and the LH side of the rear wheel, and some oversize spokes with the head cut off to use on the RH side of the rear wheel, as explained in Chapter 8. Each spoke should include a matching nipple.

Spare inner cables for brake and derailleur, with the appropriate nipple and in the length for the rear brake or derailleur, as described in the relevant chapters.

A few spare bolts with matching nuts and washers in the sizes 4, 5 and 6 mm, kept in the tire patch kit.

Spare tube in the right size and with the right valve to match your existing wheel. This is another borderline item that I rarely bother with, though others swear by it.

Spare bulbs and/or batteries for the lighting equipment on your bike. Keep bulbs wrapped up in tissue in the tire patch kit. Keep batteries in a dry place and check them at least once a month. Most people don't bother with lights, let alone spares for lights, but I consider it important.

Carrying Tools and Spares

Buy or make a pouch for the tools and small spares, along the lines of Fig. 2.7, using a sturdy fabric. Make it generous enough to fit your present tools and to allow rolling it up. Leave some slots blank for subsequent expansion. Keep this pouch in your saddle bag or handlebar bag, or tie it to the bike by means of a bungee (shock cord), e.g. against the seat stays above the rear wheel.

The pump can usually be installed alongside the seat tube. Most models nowadays fit directly between the frame tubes, providing you buy the right size. To discourage theft, either always take it with you when leaving the bike, or wrap it to the seat tube with one or two layers of adhesive handlebar tape.

Spare spokes can be tied to any one of the bike's tubes by means of adhesive handlebar tape.

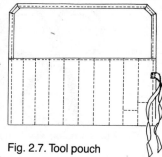
Fig. 2.7. Tool pouch

A spare tubular tire is carried under the saddle, either open or preferably in a special pouch. A spare tube will go almost anywhere, providing you wrap it up first. Even a spare tire cover of a regular wired-on tire can be carried, if it is wrapped as shown in Fig.2.8.

A spare battery must be wrapped up inside a plastic bag and stored in the side pocket of saddle bag or handlebar bag.

I suggest you equip your bike with either a saddle bag or a well supported handlebar bag to carry not only these tools, but also other items that will prove

2. Basic Tools

Fig. 2.8. Rolling up wired-on tire

handy while cycling or when you are off the bike. Don't forget to carry a lock and to use it to secure as much of the bike as possible whenever you have to leave it somewhere. Take your bag with any tools and spares along with you when you leave the bike.

Chapter 3
Preventive Maintenance

Though it will be good to know with the aid of this book you will be able to repair most problems that are likely to occur on your bike, it will be better to prevent them from occurring in the first place. That will be the subject of the present chapter. I will introduce a simple maintenance schedule that helps you keep your bike in good shape and allows you to correct problems before they get out of hand.

To do that, carry out the simple checks outlined below at the intervals stated. The tools listed in the preceding chapters are more than adequate for this purpose, providing you also get a few simple lubricants and cleaning materials:

Liquid spray lubricant, such as WD 40 or the lightest type of LPS.

Any solvent, e.g. kerosene (paraffin in Britain), mixed with about 10% mineral oil to prevent rust once the solvent dries.

Either a thick spray lubricant, heavy motor oil or a highly penetrating grease, to lubricate such items as the chain and the cables.

One or two small brushes with stiff bristles and some cleaning rags.

Daily Check

Fig. 3.1. Handlebar check

Check the following before you start out on the first ride each day you use the bike:

Tire pressure: The tires must have a pressure of at least as much as stated on the sidewall. Learn to estimate this by hand or buy a pressure gauge to match the valve used on your bike's tires.

Brakes: Each brake must grab adequately strongly to block the appropriate wheel when trying to push the bike loaded with your weight. This should happen with about a thumb-thickness of clearance between the brake handle and the handlebars. Besides, neither the brake nor the handle should be loose and the wheels must be free to turn when the brake is not applied. See Chapter 9 for adjustment and correction procedures.

Handlebars: Make sure they are tight by grabbing the front wheel between the legs while trying to twist the handlebars sideways and up-and-down, as shown in Fig. 3.1. See Chapter 4 for corrective measures.

Gears: Try to change into all possible gear combinations, holding the rear wheel off the ground and while pedalling. See Chapter 7 for any adjustments that may be required.

Lights: If your trip may take you into the hours of darkness, verify whether you are carrying at least an operating light for the front and preferably one for the rear, in addition to the big reflector for the rear.

Tools, etc.: Make sure you have all the tools and spares that seem appropriate for the length, as well as the relative remoteness and difficulty of your trip, never forgetting lock and pump.

Fig. 3.2. Lubrication points

Monthly Check

In addition to the operations listed above for the daily check, clean the bike thoroughly. Then lubricate all the points shown in Fig. 3.2 and clean off any excess lubricants.

3. Preventive Maintenance

Check whether the wheels, the cranks and the steering operate smoothly, yet without play in the bearings, and whether the wheels don't seem to wobble sideways as you slowly turn them. To check the bearings, try to move the part (e.g. the wheel) sideways relative to the bike's frame or fork – the bearings must be adjusted if it can be moved sideways.

Take a critical look at each of the components and accessories. Tighten anything that is not properly attached and replace what is no longer fully operational. Also replace or repair items that had to be adjusted or repaired frequently in the recent past and those that are obviously about to give up the ghost, such as brake cables of which individual strands have broken or tire covers that are cracked in the sidewalls or worn down smooth in patches on the tread area.

You are referrred to the subsequent chapters in this book for any repair or maintenance work needed. For more extensive overhauls or repairs that may be required, you are referred to a more comprehensive repair book or to your friendly bike shop.

While riding the bike, remain alert to the operation of your machine, listening for any suspicious irregular sounds or movements. Wobbling wheels or irregular steering, a jumping chain, rattling parts – these all are telltale signs that something is amiss. With the aid of the troubleshooting guide in the back of the book and the instructions in the various subsequent chapters, you should be able to correct most of the problems that occur.

Whenever you find you can not solve the problem, you will be well advised not to ignore the symptoms. Something is amiss and you will not be able to cycle as effectively and enjoyably as you could with a properly functioning bike. Go see a bike shop, explaining as accurately as you can what the problems or the symptoms are, if you don't want to get involved in the subject of bicycle maintenance more deeply than what is necessary to help yourself *en-route*.

Working on the Bike

Many operations on the bike – both for regular maintenance and on-the-road repairs – are most easily carried out by placing the bike upside-down, as-

3. Preventive Maintenance

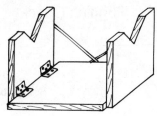

Fig. 3.3. Handlebar support stand

suming you don't have access to a repair stand that raises the machine off the ground. When turning over the bike, make the necessary provisions to assure the brake cables or any items mounted on the handlebars are not bent or damaged.

Bikes with drop handlebars and 'aero' brake levers, with hidden brake cables, present no problem. On a bike with flat handlebars, such as a mountain bike, it will suffice to loosen the attachment of the shifters and twist them out of the way. Other types of bikes with drop handlebars require you raise the handlebars off the ground by about 5 cm (2 in). This can be done by means of blocks of wood, a special stand, such as the one shown in Fig. 3.3, or with the aid of provisional measures.

Chapter 4
Steering Problems

Suppose you're out riding your bike and you find turning the handlebars does not have the desired effect. Perhaps the steering is too loose, resulting in unreliable steering or strong vibrations at higher speed. Or the handlebars slip, to turn either sideways or rotating in the vertical plane when you apply force to them, e.g. when braking. Or you find the handlebars are too high, too low or under the wrong angle. Or perhaps you fall off the bike, resulting in a bent or broken fork or handlebars.

These are the problems that will be addressed in the present chapter. If you are in doubt what is the nature of the problem, since you can identify the symptoms but not the cause, you may refer to the troubleshooting table in the Appendix. For any kind of problem, you will find a list of the possible causes and the steps to be taken for their correction. Those steps are outlined in the remaining chapters.

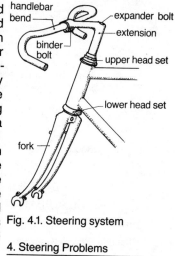

Fig. 4.1. Steering system

4. Steering Problems

The Way it Works

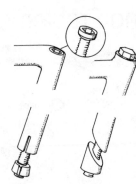

Fig. 4.2. Handlebar and stem

Tighten or Adjust Handlebar Height

The steering system is the assembly of parts that keeps the bike on track and balanced, by allowing the rotational plane of the front wheel to pivot relative to the rest of the bike. As shown in Fig. 4.1, it comprises the fork, headset bearings, handlebar stem or extension, and the handlebars.

The fork consists of the two blades, a fork crown and the round steerer tube or fork shaft that is hidden in the frame's head tube. This steerer tube is held and pivotted by means of the headset bearings. As shown in Fig. 4.2, the handlebar stem is clamped inside the steerer tube by means of an expander bolt that is accessible from the top of the stem. The handlebars are generally clamped in the stem and held tight by means of a binder bolt. On some mountain bikes the stem forms an integral part of the handlebars, while on other models the handlebars may be held in the stem by means of a V-shaped double clamp.

When the handlebars are either too high, too low, or loose, the handlebars and/or the stem must be adjusted or tightened. Refer to Fig. 4.2 and proceed as follows, ignoring any steps that obviously do not apply to your specific problem:

Procedure

Hold the front wheel clamped between your legs, and hold the handlebars, facing the bike from the front.

2. To tighten the stem in the steerer tube, merely tighten the binder bolt, after having twisted the handlebars in the desired orientation, namely straight.

3. If the height has to be adjusted or the stem must be removed for some reason, loosen the binder bolt about 4 turns, using the wrench.

4. To loosen the clamping of the stem in the steerer tube, to remove or adjust, tap on the binder bolt with hammer or other blunt object, while raising the front wheel off the ground by the handlebars.

5. To tighten the assembly in this position, refer to step 2 above.

Note: For safety reasons, at least 65 mm (2½ in) of the stem should remain inside the steerer tube. If it is not marked correspondingly, you may consider

Tools:

Allan key or whatever other wrench fits your particular bike's expander bolt; to adjust the height, you may also need a hammer or some heavy object that will act as a substitute.

4. Steering Problems

doing it yourself to prevent accidentally withdrawing it too far.

Adjust or Tighten Handlebars in Stem

To tighten the handlebars relative to the stem, i.e. to prevent them from turning in a vertical plane, or to adjust that angle, proceed as follows, referring again to Fig.4.2:

Tools:
Wrench to fit the binder bolt that holds the stem around the handlebars, usually accessible from the back.

Procedure:
1. Hold the front wheel clamped between your legs, and hold the handlebars, facing the bike from the front.

2. If required, first loosen the binder bolt that clamps the stem around the handlebars, using the wrench.

3. Orient the handlebars in the desired position

4. Tighten the binder bolt, while holding the handlebars firmly in the required orientation.

Note: If the handlebars remain loose in the stem, you may be able to solve the problem by opening the latter up further, forcing a thin piece of sheet metal (e.g. from a discarded beverage can) between handlebars and stem, and finally retightening.

Bent Handlebars

No tools required

As the result of a fall, your handlebars may be bent out of shape. In many cases, it will be possible to straighten it by the roadside, so you can at least complete the ride. Before you do, ascertain there are no obvious cracks that are indicative of severe damage in the location of the deformation.

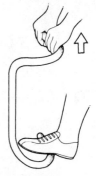

Procedure:
    Put the bike on its side with the 'good' side of the handlebars on the ground. Grab the other side and pull it up as shown in Fig. 4.3, until it has taken on its original shape. Check once more to make sure the material is not cracked – hitch a ride home if it does, and get the handlebars replaced in that case.

Fig. 4.3. Straighten handlebars

Bent or Broken Fork

In a collision, the fork will generally be the first thing to get damaged, being bent back as illustrated in Fig. 4.4. Sometimes the fork's steerer tube breaks, particularly if you have the handlebars too high on

4. Steering Problems

41

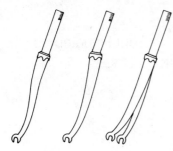

Fig. 4.4. Fork damage

too small a frame. That will probably happen during a fast descent as you hit a rock or a pothole. The effect on your own health may be more serious. If you're still fit enough to take care of such things, pick up the pieces and hitch a ride home. Let the bike shop take care of the bike's problem, replacing the fork.

Though I'd also get a bent fork replaced, it may often be straightened enough by the roadside to get you home. Examine the situation and decide which fork blade has to be bent out by how far. Find a piece of steel tubing, at least 1¼ in inside diameter and at least three feet long. The next gas station or building site may help you.

Place the bike upside-down, taking the necessary precautions not to damage anything on the handlebars. Remove the front wheel, as explained in Chapter 8. Place the steel tube over the fork blade and force the fork blade back with the leverage of the tube, countering by holding the handlebars or the whole bike down with your feet. Check to make sure there are no serious cracks in the fork blade and consult a bike shop when you get home.

The headset, shown in Fig. 4.5, consists of a double set of ball bearings. These are installed at the upper and lower ends of the head tube, with the matching parts fixed on the fork crown and screwed onto the threaded part of the steerer tube, respectively. The headset should be adjusted if the steering is either too loose or too tight. It is adjusted at the upper bearing, which is shown seperately in Fig. 4.6. Proceeded as follows:

The Headset

Fig. 4.5. Headset

Adjust Headset

Procedure

1. Loosen the big locknut on the upper headset bearing by about 3–4 turns.

2. Lift the lock washer far enough to allow turning the bearing race immediately below.

3. Tighten or loosen the adjustable race as required, by turning it clockwise or counterclockwise, respectively.

4. Put the lock washer in place and tighten the locknut, while holding the adjustable race.

Tools:
Big wrench, to fit the locknut on the top of the upper headset.

4. Steering Problems

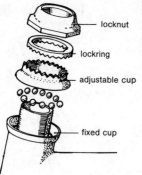

locknut

lockring

adjustable cup

fixed cup

5. If problems persist, see a bike shop for lubrication or part replacement, or learn to do it yourself with the aid of a more comprehensive bicycle repair book.

Fig. 4.6. Adjust headset

Chapter 5
Saddle Problems

The saddle is held by means of a seat post (called seat pin or seat pillar in Britain), which in turn is clamped in the bike's seat tube at the seat lug. Fig. 5.1 shows the essential componets, while Fig. 5.2 illustrates some of the most common types of seat posts in more detail. This chapter shows what little may ever have to be done along the way to eliminate any hardships the saddle may be giving you.

Most seat problems are solved by means of tightening or adjusting either the attachment of the saddle to the seat post or that of the seat post to the seat tube. On a mountain bike at least the latter adjustment is executed simply by means of a quick-release binder bolt. On other bikes you'll need wrenches to fit the binder bolt and the other adjuster bolts.

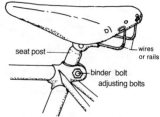

seat post

wires or rails

binder bolt
adjusting bolts

Fig. 5.1. Saddle and seatpost

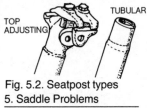

TOP ADJUSTING

TUBULAR

Fig. 5.2. Seatpost types

5. Saddle Problems

Quick-Release Binder Bolt

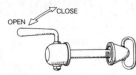

Fig. 5.3. Quick-release

Tighten Seat Post or Adjust Height

Even the quick-release, shown in Fig. 5.3, must be understood to be used correctly. The clamping mechanism only works properly if the adjusting nut on the other side is turned on just far enough when the thing is in the 'open' position to allow you to close the lever. If it is not screwed on far enough, the clamping mechanism will not hold, while you can't close the lever if it is screwed on too far. The nut can only be adjusted properly while the lever is in the 'open' position.

The seat post – and with it the entire seat – is held at the right height by clamping the split seat lug around it when the seat binder bolt is tightened. The seat post should be so long that at least 65 mm (2½ in) is held inside the seat lug for safety reasons.

To do the actual mechanical adjusting work on the saddle, first take a close look at the way it is installed on the bike, comparing it with Fig. 5.1.

Procedure:

1. Loosen the binder bolt two or three turns, to allow movement of the seat post.

2. Place the seat at the right height and orientation in a twisting motion, using the saddle for leverage, as shown in Fig. 5.4.

Tighten the binder bolt, holding the saddle in the desired position and orientation.

Note: If the seat post can not be tightened properly, its diameter is probably too small. Solve the problem temporarily by undoing the binder bolt fully, then forcing a strip of thin sheet metal (e.g. from a discarded beverage can) between seat post and seat tube, then retightening the binder bolt firmly.

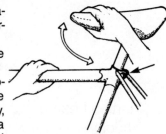

Fig. 5.4. Twist seat post

Saddle Forward Position and Angle

To tighten the saddle relative to the seat post or to change the forward position, use the seat clip that is part of the saddle on a model with the simple tubular seat post, or the adjusting bolts on a model with adjustable seat post, referring to Fig. 5.1 or 5.2.

Procedure:

1. Undo the adjustment bolts (only one bolt on some models) on your adjustable seat post or on the clip of a tubular seat post.

Tools:
Wrench to fit adjusting bolts

5. Saddle Problems

2. Once loosened, push the saddle forward or backwards until the desired position is reached.

3. Finally tighten the bolts, making sure the saddle is held under the correct position and angle relative to the horizontal plane.

Tighten Leather Saddle

This is only possible and sometimes necessary on a saddle with a self-supporting leather cover. To do this, consult Fig. 5.5 and tighten the bolt illustrated there, so the saddle cover is stretched more, giving a firmer and generally more comfortable support.

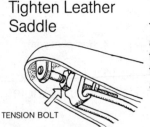

TENSION BOLT

Fig. 5.5. Tension leather saddle

Chapter 6
Drivetrain Problems

The drivetrain is the assembly of components that transfers the rider's output to the rear wheel. Though some authors also include the gearing mechanism, which is covered separately in the next chapter, my definition includes the following components:

Crankset (called chainset in Britain) with cranks, bottom bracket bearings and chainrings (also called chainwheels)
Pedals with toe-clips, if installed
The chain
Freewheel with sprockets on the rear wheel hub.

The various problems that may occur and can be treated by the roadside with simple tools shall all be outlined in the present chapter.

Crankset

The heart of the drivetrain is the crankset, which is installed in the frame's bottom bracket. It turns

Fig. 6.1. Cotterless crank

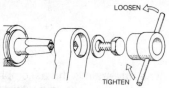

Fig. 6.2. Tighten cotterless crank

around a spindle or axle that is supported in ball bearings. The most common type is adjustable, and the adjustment will be covered below.

Tighten Cotterless Crank

<u>Tools:</u>
Wrench part of crank tool (or on models with a one-key release, merely a matching Allan key

Roadside Bicycle Repairs

The most common crankset problem is that the cranks come loose, which will be felt as an irregular pedalling movement, usually accompanied or preceded by alarming sounds. The old American one-piece crankset does not present this problem, but that type is rarely used these days. First comes the procedure for tightening the (nowadays almost universally used) cotterless crank attachment, followed by the procedure for the old fashioned cottered variety. Refer to Fig. 6.1 to see how the crank fits on the spindle and proceed as follows to tighten a crank:

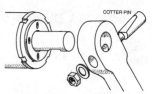

Fig. 6.3. Cottered crank

Procedure:

1. Remove the dust cap with any fitting tool (on most models a coin may be used).

2. Using the wrench part of the special crank tool, tighten the recessed bolt firmly, countering at the crank, as shown in Fig. 6.2.

3. Reinstall the dust cap.

Remark: If you have a one-key release model, the directly visible hexagonal recess bolt is merely tightened, using the crank to counter.

Fig. 6.4. Tighten

To see how this system is held together, refer to Fig. 6.3 and follow the procedure below to tighten it.

Tighten Cottered Crank

Procedure:

1. Hammer the cotter pin in a little deeper, supporting the crank on something firm and rigid with at least one of the bike's wheels raised off the ground.

2. Tighten the nut on the other side of the cotter pin, as shown in Fig. 6.4.

Tools:
Wrench to fit cotter pin nut;
Hammer or improvised
heavy object

6. Drivetrain Problems

51

Remove Cotterless Crank

This will rarely be necessary *en route*. However, you may have to do it to get at some other part for adjustment, and you have the crank tool anyway.

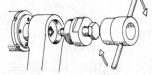

Fig. 6.5. Remove cotterless crank

Procedure:

1. Remove dust cap, as described under point 1 of *Tighten Cotterless Crank*.

2. Remove bolt, using the wrench part of the crank tool.

3. Remove the washer that lies under the bolt head.

4. Screw the other part of the crank tool into the threaded recess in the crank, making sure the inner part of the tool is retracted fully first.

5. Countering at the crank and at the body of the tool, turn in the inner part of the tool until the crank is pushed off the spindle, as shown in Fig. 6.5.

6. To reinstall, merely install washer and bolt, then proceed as described under points 2 and 3 of *Tighten Cotterless Crank*.

A bent crank can be the result of a fall with the bike. It could probably be straightened at a bike shop or garage, using the appropriate bending tool. Don't try to do it yourself with brute force, since you'd do more harm to the bike and its bearings than you'd do good to the crank.

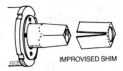

IMPROVISED SHIM

Fig. 6.6. Cotterless crank spacer

If a bent cotterless crank hits the chain stay when pedalling, you may be able to alleviate the problem temporarily by installing a spacer out of thin sheet metal (from an empty beverage can) between the tapered square spindle end and the corresponding crank hole, as shown in Fig. 6.6. This is done after you remove the crank, followed by reinstallation as described above.

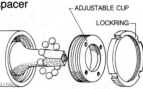

ADJUSTABLE CUP

LOCKRING

Fig. 6.7. Adjust BSA-bearing

Adjust Bearing

Described here for the common BSA-type bottom bracket bearing. See below for the American one-piece crank variety. This may be necessary if it is obviously loose, resulting in klonking noises and an irregular movement, or if it should be too tight, resulting in high resistance when pedalling. The adjustment is carried out from the LH side of the crankset,

6. Drivetrain Problems

Tools:

If you don't carry the special (big) tools for this job, a blunt srewdriver and a blunt pin

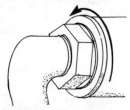

Fig. 6.8. Adjust one-piece crank bearing

One-Piece Crank

Tools:
Crescent wrench;

where the adjustable cup and the lockring are visible under the crank, as shown in Fig. 6.7.

Procedure:

1. Loosen the lockring about one turn, by turning to the left, using the hammer and the screwdriver in the slots.

2. Loosen or tighten the adjustable cup, using hammer and pin on the round recesses.

3. Tighten the lockring again, and verify that the adjustment is correct now, repeating the procedure if necessary.

Refer to Fig. 6.8 for the adjusting detail of this kind of crank, which is still used on some heavier American bikes.

Procedure:

1. Countering at the crank, unscrew the big locknut between the LH crank and the bottom bracket, which has LH thread, turning *to the right* by about two turns.

2. Lift the lock washer under the locknut

3. Tighten (turning to the left) or loosen (to the right) the cone that lies under the lock washer.

4. Retighten the locknut, then check for correct operation and readjust if necessary.

The chainrings or chainwheels – one, two or three, depending on the number of gears your bike has – are attached to the RH crank. On the simplest bikes they are merely swaged on, and when those should come loose there's nothing you can do about it short of replacing the entire combination of crank and chainring. On more sophisticated bikes they are held on an extension spider on the crank by means of screws, as shown in Fig. 6.9. Check these from time to time to make sure they are tight, countering the screw from the opposite side.

If your front derailleur gives you headaches, one cause may be that the chainrings are either loose or bent. Tightening is done by tightening the bolts shown in Fig. 6.9. To straighten, you may be able to establish where they are bent by looking along their

The Chainrings

Fig. 6.9. Chainring attachment

Fasten or Straighten Chainring

6. Drivetrain Problems

surface. Especially on bikes with three chain-wheels, the chain sometimes gets jammed between the chainrings, bending them out of shape.

Tools:
Screwdriver;
Crescent wrench

Procedure

To straighten the chainring, once you have established where it is bent in which direction, it may suffice to use a screwdriver wedged between the chainwheels. Carefully use its leverage to push the culprit back into shape. Otherwise, remove the RH crank assembly, after first placing the chain on the smallest chainring and a small sprocket in the back with the derailleur, then lifting the chain to the inside off the chainwheel.

Now proceed as shown in Fig. 6.10 to straighten individual teeth. To straighten the thing over a larger area, support it at two points and either tap on the high points with a hammer or apply force by pushing those areas down, each time holding the chainring down firmly.

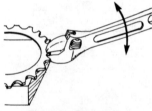

Fig. 6.10. Straighten chainwheel teeth

The Pedals

Roadside Bicycle Repairs

The pedals are installed at the ends of the cranks, being screwed on. Three things may ever have to be done to them *en route*: removal to allow transporting the bike, adjustment if they are either too loose or too tight, and getting them to work after you have fallen off the bike and the axle is bent.

Consult Fig. 6.11 for this operation, which may be necessary to transport the bike, either because the carrier insists on it or because you want to prevent damage to your bike or other articles.

Procedure:
1. For the RH pedal, grab the opposite crank to counter, and unscrew the RH pedal off by turning to the left.
2. For the LH pedal, which has LH threading, turn off *to the right*.
3. To install the pedals, screw the RH one to the right, the LH one to the left. If available (e.g. at a gas station), put some lubricant on the thread before installing, and align the thread very carefully to prevent damage to the fragile threading in the aluminum crank.

Remove and Install Pedal

Tools:
Open ended wrench or Allen key, whatever fits, the former from the front between pedal and crank, the latter from behind the crank

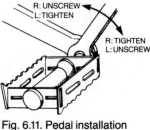

Fig. 6.11. Pedal installation

6. Drivetrain Problems

Adjust Pedal

Tools:

Pliers or wrench to remove dust cap;
Open ended wrench to match locknut;
Small screwdriver or whatever else fits the recess in the bearing cone under the locknut

Fig. 6.12. Pedal bearing adjustment

Bent Pedal Axle

Refer to Fig. 6.12 for this operation, which may make all the difference when your pedal wobbles or seems too tight.

Procedure:

1. Holding the pedal firmly, remove the dust cap.

2. Unscrew the locknut that becomes visible under the dust cap.

3. Lift the lock washer that lies under the locknut free from the adjusting cone that lies underneath.

4. Turn the cone to the left to loosen, or the right to tighten the bearing.

5. Retighten the locknut and check the operation of the pedal. Readjust if necessary.

6. When satisfied, reinstall the locknut, holding the bearing cone with the screwdriver to stop it from turning with the locknut.

The pedal axle may get bent if you fall with the bike. It will generally be impossible to do a proper roadside repair, as you will have to replace the axle. However, if the pedal can't be made to work at all anymore, you may consider stripping down the pedal until only the axle protrudes. Follow points 1 to 4 in the preceding description, but remove the various bearing parts completely, also catching the bearing balls. See whether you can get the axle straightened in a garage or other workshop, after which you can reassemble the pedal in reverse order. Even if that can't be done, leaving only the axle protrude at least allows you to ride the bike after a fashion.

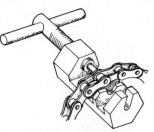

Fig. 6.13. Use of chain tool

The Chain

The chain connects the crankset with the rear wheel, where a freewheel block, generally with several different size sprockets, is installed. It may be necessary to remove and reinstall the chain for some other operation, which is done as described here:

Remove or Install Chain

Procedure:

1. Place the chain on the combination small chainwheel, small sprocket by means of the derailleurs, to release its tension.

2. Place the tool on one of the pins connecting two links, as shown in Fig. 6.13, and turn it in by 6 turns.

Tools:
Chain tool

3. Turn the handle of the tool back out and remove the tool from the chain.

4. Wriggle the chain apart.

5. Reinstall the chain, routing it around the derailleur per Fig.7.2 in Chapter 7.

Note: The preceding description applies to the removal of the continuous chain for a derailleur bike. The chain for a coaster brake bike or a three-speed with hub gearing has a removable master link, which can be removed and re-installed as shown in Fig. 6.14.

Chain 'Jumps'

This problem often occurs when a new chain or a new freewheel is installed on a bike. That's why these parts should preferably be replaced together. Either way, it will happen mainly when the gear is engaged that puts the chain on the smallest sprocket. Eliminate the problem by limiting the range of your derailleur so as never to engage that particular gear. How that is done is described in Chapter 7, *Gearing Problems*.

If it is due to an old chain on new sprockets, you may be able to alleviate the problem by removing the chain and reversing it, so that the chain wraps around the sprockets the opposite way. The reason is that chains wear asymmetrically, and the length wrapping it in the opposite direction will be slightly different as a result. Mark the inside of at least one link to make sure you know which way round it should go when reinstalling, namely so that this side is on the outside. It may not work, but it's worth trying if you have a long trip ahead of you.

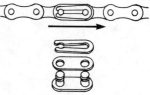

Fig. 6.14. Master chain link

Freewheel Block

Sometimes this device refuses to do what gives it its name: allow the rear wheel to rotate freely without also turning the cranks. In most instances a road-side repair is not successful, but you can try pouring oil (obtained from a discarded can at any gas station) in from the outside, as shown in Fig. 6.15, rotating the freewheel meanwhile. Keep pouring it in until it comes out clean the other side, catching it in a container, so it does not pollute the environment. Wipe off the mess after you have finished.

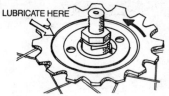

LUBRICATE HERE

Fig. 6.15. Lubricate
freewheel

Amongst the various freewheels available, I recommend using one that can be easily removed from the (special) hub, such as the Maillard Helico-Matic. It is sometimes helpful if you can remove the thing, e.g. to replace a spoke. At the roadside, this is otherwise well nigh impossible with most makes and models. If you have bought a hub and matching freewheel of this type, you merely remove the wheel (explained in Chapter 8), after which you hold it firmly, while unscrewing the freewheel with the special tool supplied with it. It can be reinstalled by hand, merely making sure the threaded parts are aligned properly.

Chapter 7
Gearing Problems

Virtually all bikes sold these days are equipped with derailleur gearing for either 10-, 12-, or 15-speed gearing. Consequently, most of this chapter will be devoted to solving the problems these systems present. In addition, you will find adjustment and emergency procedures for three-speed hub gearing.

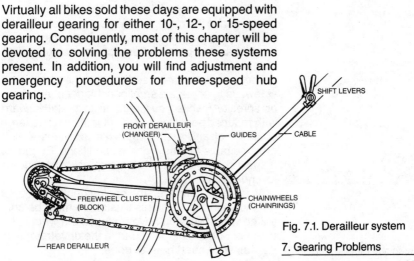

SHIFT LEVERS

FRONT DERAILLEUR (CHANGER)

GUIDES

CABLE

FREEWHEEL CLUSTER (BLOCK)

CHAINWHEELS (CHAINRINGS)

REAR DERAILLEUR

Fig. 7.1. Derailleur system

7. Gearing Problems

The Derailleur System

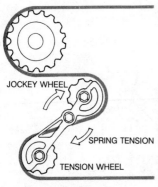

JOCKEY WHEEL

SPRING TENSION

TENSION WHEEL

Fig. 7.2. Chain routing

A typical derailleur system is shown in Fig. 7.1. It consists of a front changer and a rear derailleur, which are operated by means of shift levers. The shifters may be installed either on the down tube, at the handlebar stem or, in case of a bike with flat handlebars, on top of the bars. The shift levers are connected to the changers by means of flexible cables that run over guides and, in the case of stem and handlebar mounted shifters, partly inside flexible outer cables.

The derailleurs are used to shift the chain over sideways to engage a smaller or bigger chainwheel or sprocket, while you continue to pedal forward with reduced pedal force. A combination with a large chainwheel and a small sprocket provides a high gear, suitable for easy terrain conditions. Engaging a small chainwheel and a large sprocket provides a low gear.

At the rear derailleur, the chain should be routed as shown in Fig. 7.2. This illustration must be consulted whenever you have replaced the wheel, the chain or some other vital part in the drivetrain, until you know by heart how it's done.

Before you get down to adjusting, and in fact also during your monthly maintenance check per Chapter 3, do the following:

Keep the derailleurs themselves, as well as the chain and the various sprockets, chainwheels and control cables, clean and lightly lubricated.

Adjust the cables so that they are just taut, but not under tension, when the shift lever is pushed forward and the derailleur engages the appropiate gear.

Keep the tension screw on the shift levers tightened to give positive shifting without excessive tightness or slack.

Derailleur Care

Adjust Derailleur

The most likely thing to go wrong with your derailleur system is that one of the mechanisms either pushes the chain too far sideways, off the last chainring or sprocket, or not far enough, so it does not reach the extreme gear. Either problem is solved by adjusting the derailleur or changer mechanism, as described below, referring to Fig. 7.3.

7. Gearing Problems

Procedure:

1. Establish where the problem lies: front or rear derailleur, shifted too far or not far enough, on the inside or the outside?

2. If necessary, place the chain back on the sprocket or chainwheel, selecting a gear that combines a small chainring with a small sprocket.

3. Find the adjustable set-stop screws on the particular derailleur mechanism, which are installed in different locations on different models.

4. Determine which of the set-stop screws governs movement limitation in the appropriate direction. On many models these screws are marked with H and L for high and low gear, respectively. If not, establish yourself which is the appropriate screw by observing what happens at the ends of the screws as you shift towards the extreme gears. The high range set-stop screw is the one towards which an internal protrusion moves as you shift into the highest gear with the appropriate derailleur shift lever.

5. Unscrew the set-stop screw slightly (perhaps half a turn at a time) to increase the range if the ex-

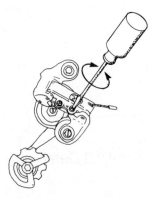

Fig. 7.3. Adjust derailleur

treme gear could not be reached. Tighten it a little if the chain was shifted beyond that last sprocket.

6. Check all possible gear combinations to establish whether the system works properly now, and fine-tune the adjustment if necessary.

Note: If the problem is obviously not caused by the set-stop screw adjustment, it will be due to excessive or insufficient tension on the cable, which can easily be verified by checking whether the cable is taut but not excessively so in the extreme gears. If not, follow the next instruction.

Adjust Cable Tension

Carry out this operation when the derailleur adjustment as described above does not solve your problem.

Procedure:
1. Set the derailleur and the chain in the gear corresponding to the released spring tension: always the smallest sprocket in the rear, on most models the smaller chainring in the front.

Tools:
Wrench to fit cable clamp bolt at derailleur;
Needle nose pliers

7. Gearing Problems

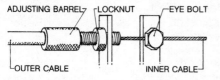

Fig. 7.4. Cable adjuster

2. Make sure the shift lever is in the corresponding released position.

3. If a cable adjusting device, as shown in Fig. 7.4, is present at the derailleur, use it to adjust the cable tension: back off the locknut, screw the adjusting barrel in or out as required, and tighten the locknut again, holding the adjusting barrel to stop it from turning with it.

4. If there is no such adjusting mechanism, or if its range is insufficient to solve the problem, loosen the cable clamping bolt on the derailleur, Pull the cable into the clamping bolt to the right location to keep it just taut, then tighten the bolt again.

5. Check all the gears and carry out any additional adjustments of cable tension or of the set-stop screws as required.

If you don't carry a spare inner cable with you to replace the one that is broken, the rear derailleur will
spontaneously shift to the highest gear (smallest
sprocket), which may be too high a gear for comfort.
In that case, follow the instruction above for adjusting, except that you screw in the high range limit
screw far enough to limit the range to engage whatever is the highest you can handle continuously.

If you do carry the right spare inner cable, with the
appropriate end nipple (check against the one installed at the shift lever), proceed as follows to replace:

Procedure:

1. Set both derailleurs and the chain in the position with the smallest sprocket and chainwheel.

2. Undo the cable clamping bolt at the derailleur
and pull the cable out, working from the nipple for
the section that attaches to it. Observe over which
guides and other parts the cable is routed, so you
can replace it correctly later. Catch any loose pieces

Tools:
Wrench to fit cable clamp
bolt at derailleur;
Pliers

7. Gearing Problems

of outer cable and other parts that may have been used, noting their locations.

3. If you have a lubricant available (grease or vaseline), first smear some all over the new cable to reduce its friction and to prevent corrosion.

4. Pull the shift lever over all the way and insert the cable until the nipple is seated in its recess at the shift lever.

5. Route the cable just like the old one was routed and attach it loosely at the derailleur by means of the clamp bolt.

6. If a cable adjusting mechanism is installed, turn it all the way in, following the instructions above.

7. Pull the cable just taut and tighten the cable clamping bolt at the derailleur.

8. Check all the gears and make any additional adjustments with set-stop screws and cable adjuster that may be required.

9. Cut off the protruding end of the cable to a length of about 3 cm (a little over 1 in), only if your pliers are really sharp (otherwise wait until you get to a shop that is appropriately equipped).

If a three-speed hub does not operate properly, it can also be adjusted quite easily. Before you try to do that, though, make sure the cable runs freely and is not pinched anywhere. Then verify whether all the guides over which it runs are attached to the bike properly, so they don't slip under tension. Refer to Fig. 7.5.

No tools required

Procedure:

1. Set the shift lever in the position for the highest gear (usually marked with the number 3).

Either pedal back half a revolution or lift the rear wheel off the ground and pedal forward, as will be required for a model with built-in coaster brake. This should engage the appropriate (i.e. highest) gear if the adjustment is correct.

3. Check the cable tension near the point where it attaches to the operating mechanism at the hub: it must be just taut but not under tension. The slightest movement of the shift lever should also start moving the little chain or the bell crank mechanism to which the cable is attached at the hub.

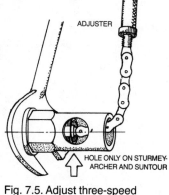

Fig. 7.5. Adjust three-speed

7. Gearing Problems

71

4. Use the cable tension adjustment mechanism (following the description for derailleur cable adjustment above), until the cable tension is correct and each gear is engaged as selected.

Chapter 8
Wheel Problems

Fig. 8.1 shows a typical bicycle wheel with regular wired-on tires. The latter consist of a separate inner tube and a cover that is held tight in a deep bedded metal rim by means of metal wires in the side of the tire cover. The other components of the wheel are hub and spokes. Some bikes use a tubular tire, also referred to as sew-up in the US or tub in Britain, which must be mounted on a slightly different rim. Wheel problems are perhaps the most common category of incidents while touring, and their repair will be covered in some detail below.

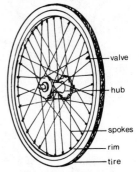

Fig. 8.1. Parts of the wheel

Remove and Install Wheel

Simple though this is, doing it right requires some basic guidelines which are given here. Wheels may be either installed with a quick-release, as used almost exclusively on ten-speeds, or by means of

Fig. 8.2. Axle nut attachment

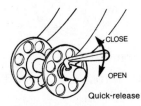

CLOSE

OPEN

Quick-release

Fig. 8.3. Quick-release
Roadside Bicycle Repairs

axle nuts. Refer to Fig. 8.2 and 8.3 for wheels with axle nuts and quick-release, respectively.

Procedure:

1. On rear wheel, first place the chain with de-railleur on the smallest sprocket and smaller chain-wheel, to minimize tension on the chain.

2. Release tension of the brake, either by means of the brake's quick-release tensioner or by backing off on the adjustment or by lifting out the cable.

3. On a wheel with axle nuts, undo both by screw-ing them to the left about three turns. On a wheel with quick-release, move the lever into the 'open' position, and only loosen the thumb nut at the other end if the wheel does not come free otherwise.

4. On a rear wheel, hold back the derailleur and the chain as shown in Fig. 8.4.

5. Raise the bike (unless it's held upside down), and remove the wheel.

6. To install, proceed in reverse order, makings sure you place the washers of a wheel with axle nuts between the nut and the fork-ends or drop-outs, and holding back the rear derailleur to allow the sprocket

to return to its proper position and the chain to wrap around it as shown in Fig. 7.2 in Chapter 7.

7. Hold the wheel exactly aligned in the center between the fork blades or stays. Tighten the axle nuts, countering at the other one, or tension the quick release by putting lever in 'closed' position – after retightening the thumb nut if you should have loosened it under point 3 above.

8. Retension the brake and make any other adjustments that may be necessary. Sometimes, if the brakes are too tight, you have to let the air out of the tire – that should be a last resort, after which it should be inflated properly again.

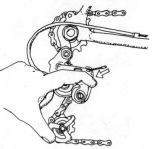

Fig. 8.4. Hold back derailleur

Tires and Tubes

The tube is inflated by means of a valve, several trypes of which are illustrated in Fig. 8.5. By far the most suitable is the Presta valve, which requires much less force to inflate properly, though it can't be done by means of a gas station air hose, unless you have the appropriate adaptor nipple. Unscrew the round nut at the tip of a Presta valve before inflating, and tighten it again afterwards. Inflation pressure is

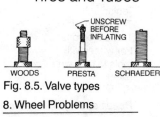

Fig. 8.5. Valve types

8. Wheel Problems

75

the key to low rolling resistance and immunity to puncturing. Maintain at least the pressure quoted on the tire sidewall, and don't hesitate to inflate at least the rear wheel by about 20percent more than that minimum value. On the road, use a hand pump and occasionally check the pressure with the aid of a tire pressure gauge.

Fixing a Flat

The flat or puncture, as it is called in Britain, is probably the most frequently encountered bike problem. Though some people despair, it really is a very simple repair, that will be outlined below for the regular wired-on tire.

Tools:
Tire patch kit;
Three tire irons;
For wheel with axle nuts: tools to take wheel out of bike

Roadside Bicycle Repairs

76

Procedure:
1. Remove the wheel from the bike. On a rear wheel, first select the gear with the small chainwheel and sprocket, then hold the chain with the derailleur back as shown in Fig. 8.4.
2. Check wether the cause is visible from the outside. In that case, remove it and mark its location, so you know where to work.

3. Remove the valve cap and locknut, unscrew the round nut (if you have a Presta valve).

4. Push the valve body in and work one side of the tire into the deeper center of the rim, as shown in Fig. 8.6.

5. Put a tire iron under the bead on that side, at some distance from the valve, then use it to lift the bead over the rim edge and hook it on a spoke, as shown in Fig. 8.7.

Fig. 8.6. Push sidewall in

6. Do the same with the second tire iron two spokes to the left and with the third one two spokes over to the right. Now the first one will come loose, so you may use it in a fourth location, if necessary.

7. When enough of the tire sidewall is lifted over the rim, you can lift the rest over by hand.

8. Remove the tube, saving the valve until last, when it must be pushed back through the valve hole in the rim.

9. Try inflating the tire and check where air escapes. If the hole is very small, so it can't be easily detected, pass the tube slowly past your eye, which is quite sensitive. If still no luck, dip the tube under water, a section at a time: the hole is wherever bub-

8. Wheel Problems

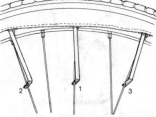

Fig. 8.7. Inserting tire irons

bles escape. Mark its location and dry the tire if appropriate. There may be more than just one hole.

10. Make sure the area around the patch is dry and clean, then roughen it with the sand paper or the scraper from the puncture kit and remove the resulting dust. Treat an area slightly larger than the patch you want to use.

11. Quickly and evenly, spread a thin film of rubber solution on the treated area. Let dry about 2 minutes.

12. Remove the foil backing from the patch, without touching the adhesive side. Place it with the adhesive side down on the treated area, centered on the hole. Apply pressure over the entire patch to improve adhesion.

13. Sprinkle talcum powder from the patch kit over the treated area.

14. Inflate the tube and wait long enough to make sure the repair is carried out properly.

15. Meanwhile, check the inside of the tire and remove any sharp objects that may have caused the puncture. Also make sure no spoke ends are projecting from the rim bed – file flush if necessary and

cover with rim tape.

16. Let enough air out of the tube to make it limp but not completely empty. Then reinsert it under the tire, starting at the valve.

17. *With your bare hands*, pull the tire back over the edge of the rim, starting opposite the valve, which must be done last of all. If it seems too tight, work the part already installed deeper into the center of the rim bed, working around towards the valve from both sides.

18. Make sure the tube is not pinched between rim and tire bead anywhere, working and kneading the tire until it is free.

19. Install the valve locknut, if appropriate for the type of valve used, and inflate the tire to about a third its final pressure.

20. Center the tire relative to the rim, making sure it lies evenly all around on both sides.

21. Inflate to its final pressure, then install the wheel. If the tire is wider than the rim, you may have to release the brake (just make sure you tighten it again afterwards). On the rear wheel, refer to point 1 above.

8. Wheel Problems

Replace Tube or Cover

Although I have rarely found it necessary while touring, some people always carry a spare tube and replace the entire thing, rather than repairing the old tube. This must also be done if the valve leaks or if the tube is seriously damaged. It is done following the relevant steps of the instructions for fixing a flat. Replacement of the tire cover is done similarly. Always make sure the rim tape that covers the spoke ends is intact.

Replace Tubular Tire

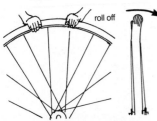

Fig. 8.8. Roll off tubular tire

That's about all you can do by the roadside if you have a problem with a tubular tire or sew-up. One good reason not to use these highly sensitive and rather expensive goodies. Consider equipping your bike with wheels for wired-on tires (often incorrectly referred to as clincher wheels in the US) if you have frequent flats or other problems with your tubular tires. To replace a defective tubular tire, first remove the wheel from the bike, as explained in a previous section of this chapter.

Removal:

1. Remove the cap from the valve, then unscrew the valve and push the pin in to let any remaining air out.

2. If there should be a lock valve on the valve (there should not be), remove and discard it.

3. Starting opposite the valve, push off the tire, rolling it off by hand pressure, working your way around gently in both directions towards the valve, as shown in Fig. 8.8.

4. When the tire is off over its entire circumference, take the valve out of the valve hole in the rim.

Installation:

1. If it is a new tire, first stretch it, pulling it between feet and hands, as shown in Fig. 8.9.

Fig. 8.9. Stretch tubular tire

2. Inflate the tire just enough so it does not hang limp, without putting pressure on it.

3. Place the valve through the valve hole in the rim and pull the tire around the circumference of the rim, working around both ways, applying enough force to keep it stretched.

8. Wheel Problems

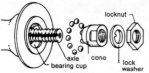

locknut

axle   cone   lock
bearing cup   washer

Fig. 8.10. Adjust hub

4. Once the entire tire is on the rim, straighten it out, so the black tread portion is perfectly centered with respect to the rim.

Note: The adhesive with which the tire is held to the rim is effective enough to hold a replacement tire, providing you don't ride around sharp curves too vigorously. Once you get home, take the thing down and apply new adhesive to the rim bed, installing the tire after it has become tacky. Repair the old tire (or have it done for you by a professional), so you can take it as a spare on your next ride.

Adjust Hub Bearings

If the wheel is loose or does not turn freely, although everything else is OK, the wheel bearing may have to be adjusted, referring to Fig. 8.10. If it is very loose and adjusting does not help, the axle may be broken, for which no roadside repair is possible – in that case, try to get to a bike shop to have the repair carried out.

If you have a wheel with axle nuts, just remove the nut on one side (in the rear, on the LH side), leaving the other one tightened. A wheel with quick-release hub should be removed from the bike. Both these operations are explained above.

Procedure:

1. Loosen the locknut (on the loosened side in case the wheel remains in the bike), countering at the underlying cone with the hub wrench, by about two turns.

2. Lift up the lock washer to free the cone somewhat.

3. Tighten or loosen the locknut by screwing it to the right or the left, respectively, countering from the opposite locknut or cone, in case the wheel was removed from the bike.

4. Retighten the locknut, countering at the cone that was adjusted.

5. Check operation of the wheel and readjust if necessary.

Tools:

Crescent wrench or open ended wrench to fit bearing locknut;
Hub wrench to fit bearing cone

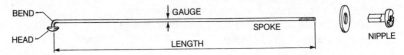

Fig. 8.11. Spoke

The Spokes

The spokes, shown in Fig 8.11, hold hub and rim together into a stressed unit. Each spoke is held to the rim by means of a screwed-on nipple. It should be kept tightened to maintain the spoke under tension, which actually prevents a lot of spoke breakages. The spokes run from the hub to the rim in one of several distinct patterns. Fig. 8.12 shows three-cross and four-cross spoking patterns – check which is used on your bike. If a spoke should break, carry out a repair according to the following description.

Replace Broken Spoke

You're in luck if it is a spoke on the front wheel or the LH side of the rear wheel, since those are adequately accessible at the hub. On the RH side of the rear wheel, on the other hand, the spoke hole in the hub is hidden by the freewheel with its sprockets. If you have a freewheel that can be easily removed,

3-cross

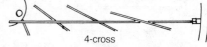
4-cross

Fig. 8.12. Spoke crossing patterns

such as the Maillard Helico-Matic, do so and follow the instructions below which apply to accessible spokes. If not, see the remark at the end of these instructions.

Procedure:

1. If necessary and possible, remove the freewheel, if the hole in the hub that corresponds to the broken spoke lies inaccessibly under the freewheel.

2. Remove the old spoke. If possible, unscrew the remaining section from the nipple, holding the latter with a wrench. If not possible, the tire must be deflated and locally lifted first, after which the nipple may be replaced by a new one.

3. Locate a spoke that runs the same way as the broken one: every fourth spoke along the circumference of the rim runs similarly. Check how it crosses

Tools:

Spoke wrench;
For inaccessible spoke: freewheel tool (or pliers to bend oversize spoke)

8. Wheel Problems

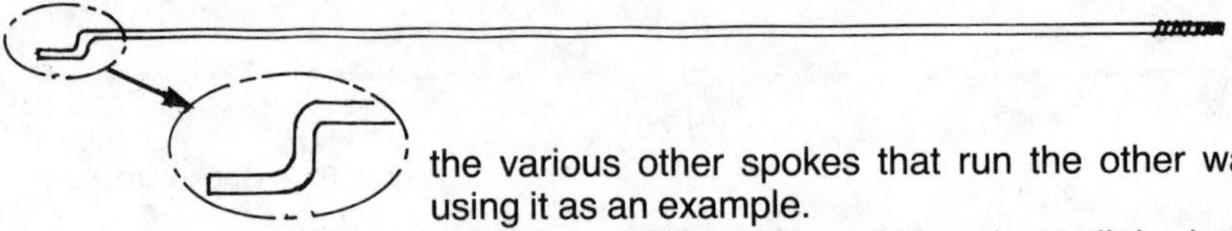

Fig. 8.13. Provisional spoke

the various other spokes that run the other way, using it as an example.

4. Thread the nipple on the spoke until the latter has the same tension as the other spokes of the wheel.

5. If the spokes do not seem to be under tension, tighten all of them half a turn at a time, until they all seem equally taut and the wheel is reasonably true. If necessary, follow the instructions for *Wheel Truing* below to correct the situation.

Note: Replace an inaccessible spoke by a temporary one. Do that by bending an overlong spoke into the shape shown in Fig. 8.13, which allows you to hook it in from between the freewheel sprocket and the hub flange. You may have to bend and rebend it several times before you have established the right size – or you may make up some spokes of the correct size at home before you leave. Replace this provisional spoke by a 'real' spoke at the bike shop upon your return.

One problem that may happen to you when touring, usually in combination with spoke breakage, is a seriously bent wheel. It will wobble sideways and rubs against the brake or other parts of the bike intermittently. Before doing anything about the rim, replace any broke spokes. Then proceed as shown here, and as illustrated primarily in Fig. 8.14.

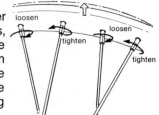

A small local dent, usually the result of riding over a sharp protrusion with inadequately inflated tires, can sometimes be relieved provisionally: remove the wheel and place the rim with the 'good' side on a level firm surface. Hammer the dent out from the other side. Get the job done properly at the bike shop when you return home – usually by replacing the entire rim.

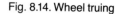

Fig. 8.14. Wheel truing

Wheel Truing

If the problem is a really serious one, the wheel looking more like a pretzel, first straighten the thing roughly. Do that with the wheel removed from the bike. Support it in its two low points, e.g. against the ground and a tree or post, while pushing against it in the high points, as shown in Fig. 8.15. Push and

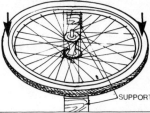

Fig. 8.15. Straighten wheel roughly

Tools:
As for 'Remove Cotterless Crank'; plus the other part of the crank tool

check and push again, until the thing begins to look like a wheel and none of the spokes seem to be excessively loose. Then proceed to the truing operation outlined below.

Procedure:
1. Check just where it is offset to the left, where to the right, by turning it slowly while watching at a fixed reference point, such as the brake shoes. Mark the relevant sections.

2. Tighten LH spokes in the area where the rim is off-set to the RH side, while loosening the ones on the LH side – and vice versa.

3. Repeat steps 1 and 2 several times, until the wheel is true enough not to rub on the brakes. This will get you by but, unless you are quite good at it, I suggest you get the job done properly by a bike mechanic as soon as possible.

Chapter 9
Brake Problems

There are four different types of rim brakes in common use, referred to as centerpull, sidepull, cantilever, and cam-operated brakes, as shown in Fig. 9.1. In addition, some simple bicycles are still equipped with a coaster brake built in the rear hub. Since the latter type, whatever its dismerits, is quite trouble-free, the instructions in this chapter will deal primarily with the adjustment and repair operations for the various kinds of rim brakes.

Compare the brakes used on your bike with those shown in the illustration, to verify which type is used. On the sidepull brake, the brake arms pivot around the attachment bolt, while they pivot around separate bosses installed on a common yoke on the centerpull brake and on the regular cam-operated brake. On the cantilever brake and the frame-mounted variety of the cam-operated model, the pivots are installed on bosses that are attached di-

Fig. 9.1. Brake types

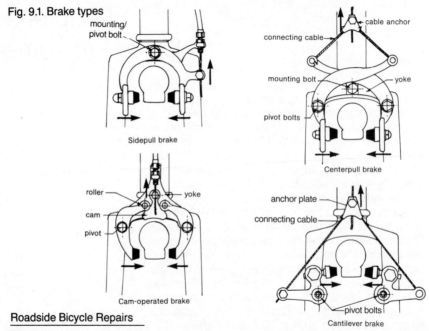

Sidepull brake

Cam-operated brake

Centerpull brake

Cantilever brake

rectly to the fork or seat stays, which must be welded on in those locations.

With any rim brake, the force applied by pulling the lever is transmitted to the brake unit by means of flexible cables. These cables are partly contained in flexible outer cables and restrained at anchor points on the frame. Usually a quick-release mechanism is built in somewhere along the way to release the cable tension, so the wheel may be removed from the brake and to ease work like replacing or adjusting the cable.

The force is transmitted from the handle to the parts of the brake unit to which the cable is attached. A pivoting action then pulls the ends of the brake arms with the brake blocks against the sides of the rim to create the drag that slows down the bike. When the brake does not work satisfactory, the cause can be in any element of the chain of power from lever, over cable and anchors, via the brake mechanism and the brake blocks to the bicycle wheel's rim.

All brakes have an adjustment mechanism to shorten the cable, which allows you to apply suffi- 9. Brake Problems cient force without the thing bottoming out. It may be installed at the handle, at the brake unit or at one of the cable anchor points. The adjustment is described below. Brake cables should not be elastic or 'spungy', to allow applying adequate force. Brake cables should be routed as short as possible, providing they are not forced in excessively tight bends in any position of handlebars or brake.

Brake Check

To make sure the brakes work properly, it is enough to test them at low speed. Try them out separately at walking speed, which is perfectly safe and still gives a representative test of the deceleration reached with each brake. Used singly while riding the bike at walking speed, the rear brake must be strong enough to skid the wheel when the lever is applied firmly. The front brake should decelerate the bike so much that the rider notices the rear wheel lifting off when it is fully applied. If their performance is inadequate, carry out the adjustment described below.

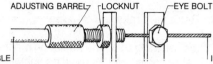

ADJUSTING BARREL — LOCKNUT — EYE BOLT

OUTER CABLE

INNER CABLE

Fig. 9.2. Cable adjuster

Adjust Brake

We will assume the brake must be adjusted because its performance is insufficient. In this case, the cable tension must be increased by decreasing its length. Should the brake touch the rim even when not engaged, the opposite must be done to lenghten the cable slightly. The adjuster mechanism is shown in Fig. 9.2.

Before starting, check to make sure the brake blocks lie on the rim properly over their entire width and length when the brake is applied, as shown in Fig. 9.3. Ideally, the front of the brake block should touch the rim just a little earlier than the back. If necessary, adjust by loosening the brake block bolt, moving the block as appropriate. Retighten it while holding the brake block in the right position. If necessary, the brake block may be replaced when you get to a bike shop, after which the adjustment steps that follow must be carried out as well.

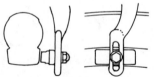

Fig. 9.3. Brake block alignment

9. Brake Problems

93

Tools:
Often none;
sometimes wrench to fit
brake cable attachment bolt
and brake block bolt

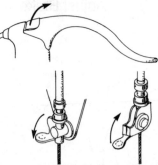

RELEASE IN DIRECTION OF ARROWS

Fig. 9.4. Brake quick-release

Center Brake

Procedure:

1. Release brake quick-release, as shown in Fig. 9.4.

2. Loosen locknut on the adjusting mechanism for the brake cable, which may be installed on the brake, on the handle or at a cable anchor point.

3. While holding the locknut, screw the barrel adjuster out by several turns; then tighten the quick-release again.

4. Check the brake tension: the brake must grab the rim firmly when a minimum of 2 cm (¾ in) clearance remains between the brake handle and the handlebars.

5. If necessary, repeat steps 1–4 until the brake works properly.

6. Tighten the locknut again, while holding the adjusting barrel to stop it from turning.

If the rim brake rubs on one side of the rim, even though the wheel is adjusted correctly and the problem remains after adjusting the brake, the brake's mounting bolt must be twisted. On a centerpull brake that is easy enough: merely twist the entire yoke on which the brake pivots are installed.

To do this on a sidepull brake, some manufacturers provide special tools, which should be used as appropriate. If no special tool is available, twist the mounting bolt by simultaneously turning the nut in the rear of the brake attachment and one of the two nuts on top of the brake in the apprpriate direction. When turning to the right, pick the outermost nut; when turning to the left the one underneath, as shown in Fig. 9.5.

If the brake cannot be made to operate properly, despite all efforts to adjust, the problem may be caused by excessive friction or looseness in one of the mechanical elements. Proceed as follows to identify and alleviate the cause:

Procedure:
1. Check whether all attachment bolts are tightened and none of the parts are either bent or otherwise inoperative.

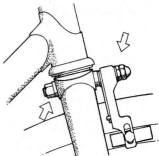

Fig. 9.5. Center sidepull brake

Brake System Repair

Tools:
Wrench;
Pliers;
Sometimes: lubricant

9. Brake Problems

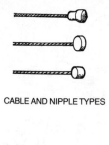

CABLE AND NIPPLE TYPES

Fig. 9.6. Cable damage

2. Push the brake blocks against the rim by pushing in the brake arms and let them come back. If they can't be pushed together or don't return under the spring's force alone, the brake mechanism itself is at fault. Use oil at the pivots, try to free the individual pivot points, and straighten any parts that are bent and rub against one another.

3. If the problem persists, proceed to the cable at the brake mechanism, then check whether the inner cable is free to move relative to the outer cable. If not, try lubricating the inner cable where it enters the outer cable and runs through or over guiding parts. If that doesn't help, disassemble the cable and use the pliers to work on any protrusions on the outer cable on which the inner cable may have hung up.

4. If the cable works, while the problem persists, try out the lever. If it does not operate freely, try lubrication at the pivot, loosen or tighten the pivot bolt, and straighten out any deformed parts that may present friction.

5. Finally reassemble everything, making sure all connections are tight, all pivots are free to move,

and there are no kinks in the cable. If necessary, readjust the brake as described before.

To avoid the unsettling experience of the brake cable snapping just when it is most needed, replace it as soon as individual strands show signs of damage at the end nipple, as shown in Fig. 9.6. Since a cable may have to be replaced while you are touring, it will be smart to carry a spare. Make sure the spare cable has a nipple that matches the particular brake handle used on your bike.

Tools:
Wrench to fit cable clamp bolt;
If available, sharp cutting pliers and lubricant

Procedure:
1. Loosen the brake quick-release. On a cantilever brake, push the brake arms together and take out one of the nipples of the connecting straddle cable. On a frame-mounted cam-operated brake, push the brake arms together and twist out the cam plate.
2. Loosen the clamp or eye bolt that holds the cable at the brake, until you can free the old cable.

9. Brake Problems

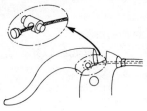

Fig. 9.7. Nipple in handle

3. Push the old cable out, working towards the handle, where you can dislodge the nipple as shown in Fig. 9.7. On a mountain bike brake handle (Fig. 9.8), turn the adjuster into such a position that the slot in the handle is free, so you can take out the cable.

4. Pull the entire inner cable out, catching the outer cable section or sections, as well as any other parts, memorizing their installation locations.

5. Lubricate the new cable. Back off on the locknut, then screw the adjusting barrel in all the way.

6. Starting at the handle, push the new cable through, securing the nipple by pulling it taut. Thread the cable through the various anchor points, outer cable sections and other parts through the adjuster.

7. Finally push the cable end through the eye bolt at the brake, and tighten the bolt loosely. Secure the nipple into the handle by pulling the cable taut from the brake end.

8. Tighten the eye bolt while continuing to keep the cable taut.

9. Adjust the cable tension, following the preceding instructions.

10. Test the brake in operation, followed by a final adjustment if necessary.

11. Finally, cut off the free end of cable until about 3 cm (1 ¼ in) projects, using sharp cutters. Wait until you get to a bike shop or garage to do that if you don't have the right tool.

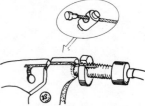

Fig. 9.8. Access at mountain bike brake handle

Coaster Brake Problems

If you ride a bike with a coaster brake, the worst that can happen is that your chain breaks or that the lever on the LH side that holds the inner life of the brake fixed to the bikes frame comes loose.

If the chain snaps, you will not be able to brake at all, and will have to steer towards a likely place to come to a standstill without serious harm to body and bike. Use your spare links and the chain tool to mend the chain, roughly following the instructions for chain assembly in Chapter 6. If you don't have spare chain links, you may be able to shorten the chain slightly and compensate for it by pushing the

9. Brake Problems

wheel further forward, not forgetting to loosen and subsequently tighten the attachment of the lever on the LH side of the hub.

If the lever comes loose, you will notice unreliable and intermittent operation, both when braking and when accelerating subsequently. Pull the lever back in the correct position and use a spare bolt to attach it firmly to the clamp around the LH chain stay.

Chapter 10
Accessory Problems

The one advantage of many accessories from a maintenance standpoint is probably the fact that they are superfluous. Consequently, they can be removed and perhaps even discarded when they cause you grief along the way. As for the (under certain circumstances) essential accessories, such as lights and luggage racks, attaching them properly and perhaps replacing their attachment hardware is the most important advice. It can't hurt to have some spare bolts, washers and nuts in your tire patch kit for such purposes.

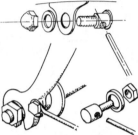

Fig. 10.1. Fender stay attachment

Fenders

If the fenders or the stays with which they are attached rub against the wheels, don't just bend the stays like wishbones to relieve the problem. Instead, loosen the attachment bolts, shown in Fig. 10.1, straighten anything that is bent, and slide

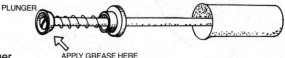

PLUNGER

Fig. 10.2. Pump plunger

APPLY GREASE HERE

the stays in such a position that the whole affair is in order, before tightening the attachement bolts.

Pump

Though more properly a tool, we'll cover the pump as an accessory here. If the thing doesn't do its job, first see whether it helps to tighten the screw-on cap at the head, where you place it on the valve. If still no luck, unscrew it and turn over and massage the thick rubber washer that lies inside, after which the cap is screwed on firmly again. Finally, you may remove the plunger from the other end of the pump barrel (see Fig. 10.2) and try greasing and kneading it.

Lock

If your lock doesn't work, lubrication often does the trick, assuming you are using the right key. Don't just pour oil (from a supposedly empty can at any gas station, if you don't carry your own) down the key hole. Instead put one or two drops on the key and about as much at the points where the shackle disappears into the lock body.

Battery Lights

If a battery light gives you trouble on the way, first check whether the bulb and the battery work when removed from the housing and connected up provisionally (any piece of wire or metal found by the roadside will do). If not, you have to replace one or the other – generally it's the battery, so make sure you carry a spare.

If bulb and battery work outside the housing but not when installed, check whether the various parts are installed properly and the bulb is screwed down firmly. Clean or bend contacts of bulb, battery, housing and switch. If no luck, don't risk riding in the dark, but hitch a ride back to civilization.

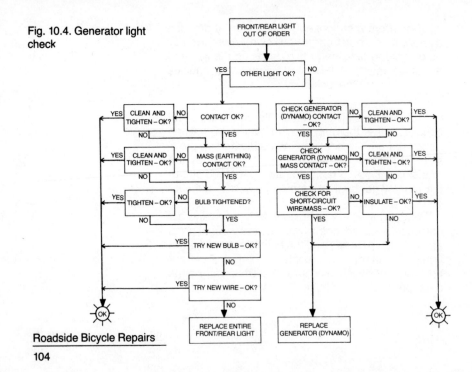

Fig. 10.4. Generator light check

Roadside Bicycle Repairs

Generator Lights

Referred to as dynamo lighting in Britain, this is a more complex and generally rather shoddily installed system. I use it nevertheless, since it provides the most effective and reliable form of illumination with a little care and understanding. Fig. 10.3 shows how the various parts are connected: single-pole insulated cables from generator contact to front and rear light contacts, and bare metal connections between the various parts and the frame for the other electric pole.

If the thing gives you trouble, go about it systematically, being guided by the simplified logic diagram Fig. 10.4. In your supply of spare part, make sure you at least have one of each of the bulbs required and preferably a length of insulated wire. That will be sufficient to solve at least 90% of your lighting problems.

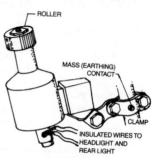

Fig. 10.3. Generator lights

Appendix

Problem/symptom	Possible cause	Remedy	Page
high resistance (pedalling and coasting)	1. insufficient tire pressure	inflate tire, fix flat	32, 76
	2. tire rubs on frame or accessory	adjust or straighten	87, 101
	3. wheel bearing problems	adjust bearing	82
high resistance (pedalling only)	1. chain dirty, dry or worn	clean, lubricate	59
	2. bottom bracket problems	adjust, lubricate	53f
	3. chainwheel rubs on frame	adjust, tighten, straighten	55
bike pulls to one side	1. wheel misaligned	adjust, center, straighten	73, 87f
	2. front fork bent	straighten fork	41
bike vibrates	1. wheels not true	true (straighten) wheel	87f
	2. headset loose	adjust headset	43
	3. hub or bearings loose	tighten, adjust	73, 82
chain 'jumps'	1. sprocket worn	limit derailleur range	65, 69
	2. chain worn or loose	adjust or reverse chain	60
	3. stiff or damaged link	free link by twisting chain	59

Problem/symptom	Possible cause	Remedy	Page
chain drops off chainwheel or sprocket	1. derailleur problems 2. chainwheel loose or bent 3. chain loose	adjust derailleur range tighten or bend chainwheel shorten chain or move wheel back	65 59, 73
irregular pedalling movement	1. crank, bottom bracket, pedal loose 2. crank or pedal axle bent	tighten or adjust get straightened, strip pedal	50, 53 57 52, 58
gears do not engage properly	1. derailleur or 3-speed problems 2. gear control problems 3. chain too loose or tight	clean adjust, fasten or free clean, lubricate, free, replace correct chain lenght	65, 71 65, 69 59
rim brake ineffective	1. brake out of adjustment 2. rim greasy, wet or damaged 3. brake cable pinched or corroded 4. brake or handle damaged	correct block attachment clean, straighten rim free, lubricate free lubricate	93 87, 89 97 95

Problem/symptom	Possible cause	Remedy	Page
brake jitters	1. rim damaged	straighten rim	89
	2. brake loose	adjust and tighten brake	95
	3. headset loose	adjust headset	43
rim brake squeals	1. brake block does not match rim	adjust brake block,	93
	2. rim dirty or damaged	clean, straighten rim	89
	3. brake arm loose	tighten pivot bolt	95
coaster brake ineffective	1. chain loose or broken	adjust chain, move wheel forward	59, 73
	2. brake lever loose	reinstall lever on chain stay	99
generator light defective	1. bulb defective	replace bulb	103
	2. wiring contact loose	repair connection	103
	3. mass contact ineffective	remove rust, tighten pinch screw	103
battery light defective	1. battery dead	replace by spare	102
	2. switch contact ineffective	clean and bend into contact	102
	3. bulb defective	replace by spare bulb	102

Index

Bibliography

Alexander, D., *Bicyclist's Emergency Repair*. South Passadena, CA.: Alexander & Alexander, 1986.

Ballantine, R., *Richard's Bicycle Book*. New York: Ballantine, London: Pan, 1978.

Brandt, J., *The Bicycle Wheel*. Menlo Park, CA : Avocet, 1981.

Coles, C. W., and Glenn, H. T., *Glenn's Complete Bicycle Manual*. New York: Crown Publishers, 1973.

Cuthberson, T., *Anybody's Bike Book*. Berkeley, CA: Ten-Speed Press, 1984.

–, *The Bike Bag Book*. Berkeley, CA: Ten-Speed Press, 1981.

DeLong, F., *DeLong's Guide to Bicycles and Bicycling*. Radnor, PA.: Chilton Books, 1978.

Sloane, E., *Eugene A. Sloane's Complete Guide to All-Terrain Bicycles*. New York: Simon & Schuster 1985.

Sutherland, H., etc., *Sutherland's Handbook for Bicycle Mechanics*. Berkeley, CA: Sutherland Publications, 1983.

Van der Plas, R., *The Bicycle Repair Book*. San Francisco: Bicycle Books, 1985.

–, *The Mountain Bike Book*. San Francisco: Bicycle Books, 1984.

–, *The Penguin Bicycle Handbook*. Harmondsworth (GB): Penguin Books, 1983.

Whiter, R., *The Bicycle Manual on Maintenance and Repairs*. Chicago, IL: Contemporary Books, 1972.

Roadside Bicycle Repairs

About the Author

Rob van der Plas is a professional engineer and a lifelong bicyclist. He has both raced and toured by bicycle extensively in Europe and America. For many years now he has occupied himself primarily with the technical aspects of the bicycle. In this capacity he has taught bicycle repair and maintenance courses and made numerous contributions on the subject to specialized periodicals on both sides of the Atlantic.

In addition to the present book, Bicycle Books has published several of his other works, including *The Bicycle Touring Manual, The Bicycle Racing Guide, The Mountain Bike Book,* and *The Bicycle Repair Book*. And, yes, between writing books and articles on the subject, Rob Van der Plas still finds time to ride and maintain his bike.